HAMBURGER SYNDROME
A Story Of Adult Autism

By

Dr. Kascia Hanska

2010
Parkway Publishers, Inc
Boone, North Carolina

Copyright © 2010 by Kascia Hanska

Hamburger Syndrome

All rights reserved. No part of this book may be reproduced or transmitted in any form or by any means, electronic, or mechanical, including photocopying, recording or by any information storage and retrieval system, without permission in writing from the publisher. No abridgement or changes to the text are authorized by the publisher.

Library of Congress Cataloging-in-Publication Data

Hanska, Kascia, 1947-
Hamburger syndrome : a story of adult autism / by Kascia Hanska.
p. cm.
Summary: "This book explores the issues of adult autism and uses cartoon panels to communicate the ideas"--Provided by publisher.
ISBN 978-1-59712-361-7
1. Autism--Popular works. I. Title.
RC553.A88H355 2010
616.85'882--dc22
2009031494

Printed in the United States of America by
Parkway Publishers, Inc

Order from:
Parkway Publishers, Inc
PO Box 3678
Boone, North Carolina 28607
www.parkwaypublishers.com

This book is dedicated to
the parents of individuals with autism
who deserve hope for their children
and peace for themselves.

Dr. Kascia Hanska

PREFACE

Autism officially arrived in 1943, the year it was first described by Leo Kanner as a separate disorder. Undoubtedly, however, it had been around much longer, just subsumed under the heading of other disorders. Its incidence has been rapidly on the rise in the last several years. Some part of the increase is thought to be due to the continuing awareness and refinement of classification. Another part may be due to other, as yet unidentified, factors. The bottom line is no one knows for sure what causes autism. There are theories and evidence that the cause might be a genetic variant or an environmental insult or both, which isn't saying anything specific.

It is not possible to diagnose autism with a definitive test like a blood test. But in its full blown classic manifestation of unusual symptoms, it is usually unmistakable. Starting at a young age, often less than three, and continuing throughout adulthood, there can be serious deficits in language and social relatedness, and oddities of behavior.

Although there are some very successful treatments for autism, there is no cure. When, on occasion, children appear to move beyond the diagnosis, some professionals question whether it was either a very mild form or a misdiagnosis initially.

No two children with autism are exactly alike in the specifics of their presentation or their development. Some children get worse as they age, but for many, symptoms lessen, but do not disappear. Most are left with a lifelong dependence on others – usually because of an inability to make sound decisions, to relate to others, or to secure adequate employment.

At one time, little was done for these children and many ended up institutionalized. Over the last few decades, staying at home, special educational programs in regular educational settings, and respite support became more common. Most funded programs today, however, end at age 22, leaving parents frantic about what the future holds for their children and for themselves. Group homes have replaced institutions, but these are not always the answer or choice for those with limited social skills. Also, although group homes are substantially less expensive than institutional living, there are inadequate facilities and funds available, and being on waiting lists for many years is not uncommon. A study by Easter Seals found more than eighty percent of young adults with autism (ages 19-30) live at home. In addition, most individuals on the autism spectrum are unemployed as adults or employed for only a few hours a week at minimum wages. Parents, rightfully so, worry about what will happen to their children after they reach age 22 and beyond, including after the parents have passed on or are themselves incapable of caring for their adult children.

This book, while not an answer for all individuals, is a story that might provide hope in an otherwise bleak horizon. This is the story of how an adult male with classic autism - who was dependent on others for most basic decisions, who held only part time jobs with one-on-one job coach assistance, and who needed lots of private time - was able to live in his own apartment. To protect his privacy, names and details have been altered, but the basic facts remain the same.

THIS IS A STORY ABOUT

A MAN NAMED ART.

Dr. Kascia Hanska

ART HAS LOTS OF ASSETS.

Dr. Kascia Hanska

LOTS OF THINGS WORRY ART.

Dr. Kascia Hanska

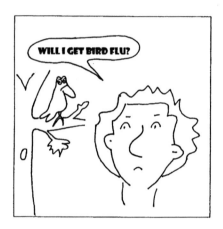

BASIC COMMUNICATION RULES

CAN BE DAUNTING

Dr. Kascia Hanska

AS CAN ENTERING INTO A CONVERSATION.

Dr. Kascia Hanska

HE SOMETIMES SPEAKS

IN IDIOSYNCRATIC WAYS

Dr. Kascia Hanska

OR SLIPS INTO CLANG ASSOCIATIONS.

Dr. Kascia Hanska

ART HAS PREOCCUPATIONS,

Dr. Kascia Hanska

BELIEFS,

Dr. Kascia Hanska

Art believed in Santa Claus until he was 22. Then he found out his grandparents didn't let his mother and her brothers believe in Santa as children.

AND RULES.

Dr. Kascia Hanska

HIS PHYSICAL PRESENTATION

CAN BE NOVEL,

Dr. Kascia Hanska

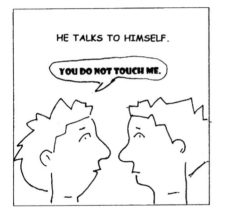

AND HE CAN

BE EGOCENTRIC.

Dr. Kascia Hanska

IN MANY WAYS,

HE IS INNOCENT,

Dr. Kascia Hanska

AND THIS NAIVETE

CAN TEMPT OTHERS.

Dr. Kascia Hanska

BUT SOMETIMES HE CAN SOUND ERUDITE.

Dr. Kascia Hanska

THIS CAN BE CONFUSING.

Dr. Kascia Hanska

ART LIVED AT HOME UNTIL HE WAS 26, THEN HE WANTED TO MOVE OUT.

Dr. Kascia Hanska

ART HAS A BIG DREAM.

Dr. Kascia Hanska

BUT WITH LOTS OF EFFORT,

IT HAPPENS.

Dr. Kascia Hanska

BECAUSE ART'S IQ TEST COMES OUT TO BE < 70, HE PASSES (OR FAILS, DEPENDING ON HOW YOU LOOK AT IT)

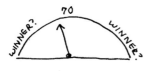

THIS QUALIFIES HIM TO BE ABLE TO HAVE A GUARDIAN (HIS FATHER) AND TO GET SSI BENEFITS. HE ALSO GETS SECTION 8 HOUSING BENEFITS (AFTER BEING ON A WAITING LIST FOR ONE YEAR).

HIS MOM FINDS A PLACE THAT IS SAFE, AFFORDABLE ($650 A MONTH, INCLUDING ALL UTILITIES), WILLING TO ACCEPT SECTION 8 FUNDING, AND ABLE TO PASS SECTION 8 FUNDING INSPECTIONS.

HIS DAD BUYS A BED FRAME AND MATTRESS, A KITCHEN TABLE AND TWO CHAIRS. HE GETS HIM A USED SOFA AND CHAIR FROM HIS UNCLE. ART ALREADY HAS A DESK, DESK CHAIR, BOOKSHELF, TV, DVD, VCR, TELEPHONE....

SAM, ONE OF HIS AIDES, GOES WITH HIM TO BUY DISHES, SILVERWARE, POTS, PANS, KNIVES, A TOASTER, COOKING UTENSILS, TOWELS, SHEETS, A COMFORTER, PILLOWS....

ART'S CONCERN:

I NEED COASTERS.

HE STILL HAS SUPPORT,

Dr. Kascia Hanska

BUT THE SCHEDULE

CAN BREAK DOWN.

Dr. Kascia Hanska

WHEN HE IS ALONE,

HE MAKES DECISIONS.

Dr. Kascia Hanska

SOMETIMES, THEY CAN

BE COSTLY.

Dr. Kascia Hanska

ART WOULD LIKE TO BE

MARRIED SOME DAY.

Dr. Kascia Hanska

IT WAS TIME TO THINK

ABOUT BIRTH CONTROL.

Dr. Kascia Hanska

IT COULD HAVE GONE EITHER WAY AT ART'S HEARING.

Dr. Kascia Hanska

THERE ARE OTHER THINGS TO THINK ABOUT IF HE GETS MARRIED.

Dr. Kascia Hanska

UNDER CT LAW, THERE ARE NO IMPEDIMENTS TO MARRIAGE. EVEN THOUGH HE HAS A GUARDIAN, HE CAN GET MARRIED AT ANYTIME.

ALL HE KNOWS IS HE WANTS TO GET MARRIED.

AND, FACE IT, HOPE IS WHAT HAS GOTTEN HIM THIS FAR.

Dr. Kascia Hanska

POSTSCRIPT

This book is not an answer. It is only the start of the journey to find an adequate way to provide a meaningful life for adults who have autism and hope for parents of children with autism who lay up at night worrying about what is to become of their child. Because this path is new or atypical, many hurdles were encountered along the way. And the end result is not without controversy.

This book focuses on Art, an adult with autism, so only an overview of what Art was like as a child is given. However, Art had many problems and there was never any question about his diagnosis. He was inconsolable as an infant, had no eye contact, never seemed to sleep, and walked on his toes; as a toddler he could recite from memory lots of information, then lost all speech at age 3. He disliked most toys and any minor changes in any routine resulted in a tantrum. In public, he drew lots of attention from others for his unusual mannerisms. The list goes on and on. He did regain his speech and show improvements over the years, but the improvements were never so great to allow removal of his autism classification. The first part of this book is evidence of this.

Art lived at home up to age 26, but he was not content. He saw his siblings and his "friends" at high school get a license, go off to college, then graduate and get their own place. He never understood why he couldn't and it bothered him that he was not "an adult." He stopped watching cartoon movies ("they were for kids"), took up drinking non-alcoholic beer (because it looked like he was holding a beer like everyone else), and refused to put on his seat-belt in the back seat of a car (because kids were required to be buckled up and in the back set of a car). But it was not enough. He wanted his own place. There is no way Art could have realized his wishes on his own. But after many years of his family working the system, it happened. Listed below are some of the major hurdles that first had to be overcome.

Hurdle #1 Funding

How do you secure enough funds to have your adult child live somewhere else? Not many people can afford to pay for a separate living space like a house or apartment, and individuals to watch over their adult child. Government funds are available but limited. It was important to have Art's IQ tested before he was 18. (An IQ < 70 helps to secure guardianship which also helps to get other services.) Also, SSI eligibility was considered as soon as possible. His state Department of Mental Retardation (a department which also goes under other names in other states: e.g. Department of Developmental Delays) provided funding for housing, employment support, and counseling. Section 8 housing and food stamps came from the federal government, and health care from the state government (although if your child is disabled, they may also be able to stay on your health care policy). No one will come to your door to offer these benefits and you will seldom get them right away just by applying for them.

Hurdle #2 Determining abilities and needs

Art could be home alone at night, but not all day long. He could microwave foods, and order take-out food to be delivered to his house. He could wash his own clothes and take care of his own hygiene. He needed help buying food, going to and being at work, and interfacing with the community in the laundromats and elsewhere. He could use a house phone and a cell phone with unlimited long distance, but paid calls had to be blocked.

Hurdle #3 Safety versus happiness

There is no question that your adult child will probably be the safest living with you. Yet for Art this arrangement was making him miserable. He had no privacy, little opportunity to be on his own, and was probably over protected, which never gave him the chance to learn from his mistakes. His family came to the conclusion that it was better for Art to live a riskier, happy life rather than a safer, miserable one, while they would do everything they could to protect him. They realized they may have been doing Art a disservice in the long run keeping him at home since they would not be around forever to help him secure services down the road. Obviously, all of this was a grand experiment which they were prepared to end if it became untenable. They had serious concerns going into it, but were willing to give it a try.

Hurdle #4 Finding competent aides

This can be a challenge no matter what environment your child lives in. Fortunately Art can express his displeasure, and can and does let others know if he doesn't like something. Of course, you still have to figure out the reality of the situation from his version. Art has had some outstanding people work with him and others not so much. Usually the ad for an aide only asks someone to "have a car and a license." No degree or specific educational training is required and little on the job training is given; most of these jobs are minimum wage, and the turn-over is high. Although Art no longer lived with his family, they needed to remain actively in the loop to monitor services.

Hurdle #5 Working with the community

Art does have down time where he walks around the community on his own. It would be obvious to anyone who met him that he is not typical. For example, he often talks to himself (although cell phone technology has made this appear more common). Most people who encounter him are kind to him or let him be. Occasionally, someone will tell him to "get lost." So far, his family has not been notified of any more negative encounters, although this is always a risk. He lives in a medium size community with a main street that has a good amount of traffic. The advantage to this is that there is a major crosswalk he can use where traffic on all four sides has to stop while a chirping noise goes off when crossing is safe. His family has made themselves known to people he is likely to encounter: for example, his landlord, the librarian, and the restaurant owners from whom he orders food delivery.

Hurdle #6 Personal relationships

Art has never really had a girlfriend although he would like to be married someday - mostly because that would make him more of an adult in his mind. Whether or not someone who cannot take full care of themselves should have children on their own seems to be a no-brainer but in fact, it is a very difficult social and legal issue you may have to face. Fortunately, his family was able to solve this one; however, the issue of sexually transmitted disease is still out there. It seems unlikely Art would ever have the opportunity; however, it is not impossible to imagine someone meeting him and offering him sex (marriage) to gain access to whatever little he has. If he got married, his family would have to deal with the fact that his funding could be cut even though he has no plans to ever live with this person. If his funding were cut, his living arrangement could be jeopardized.

The bottom line

There is no question that Art sees this as the best living arrangement for him and it is an arrangement that allows his family a degree of privacy they have not enjoyed since he was born. The cost is vigilance and a willingness to address the inevitable problems that will occur. They see this as a small price for a huge gain, one they once thought unimaginable.

Acknowledgements

    I would like to gratefully thank Steve Narmontes and Rao Aluri - this work would not exist but for their much appreciated assistance - and my husband for his love and support of me and his love of and devotion to his children and grandchildren.

Readers' Comments

    I loved it. Hanska's young adult autistic man is pictured with realism, love, and humor. Autism is nothing to laugh at, but Art's characteristic take on things, his interactions with others and his innocence are presented with such humor, he becomes totally endearing to the reader. Hanska offers a working model of how to let adult individuals with autism gain their independence by illustrating how Art's parents were first able to secure a support system and then let go -- with vigilance.
  - Julie Peck,
  Caregiver, Parent Advocate, Recipient of State-Wide Human Rights Award

    Hanska draws a realistic picture of a person with autism trying to be an adult in the "real" world. Using cartoons, she quickly captures the attention of the reader as she enters into the life of a family dealing with autism. The transition to adult services is just beyond so many parents. They think that some agency in the sky will take care of the issues. Hanska illustrates the battles they will inevitably have to face.
  - Lois Lynch
  Special Education Administrator

    Kascia Hanska has written a terrific little book about autism. Funny, sad, and informative, this book provides an interesting and engaging way to learn about options for adults with developmental disabilities.
  - Chris Hakala,
  Psychology Professor

CPSIA information can be obtained at www.ICGtesting.com
Printed in the USA
LVOW100306100513

333169LV00001B/173/P